21st Century Skills Library

GLOBAL PRODUCTS

SKATEBOARDS

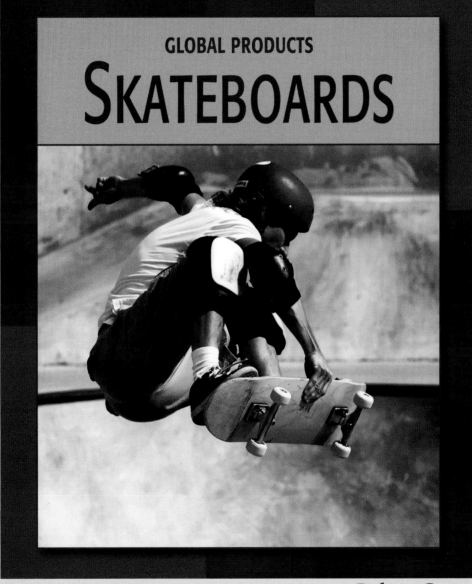

Robert Green

Cherry Lake Publishing
Ann Arbor, Michigan

CHERRY
LAKE
Publishing

Published in the United States of America by Cherry Lake Publishing
Ann Arbor, MI
www.cherrylakepublishing.com

Content Adviser: Jim Fitzpatrick, Vice President, USA Skateboarding

Photo Credits: Pages 7 and 17, © Steve Boyle/New Sport/Corbis

Map by XNR Productions Inc.

Library of Congress Cataloging-in-Publication Data
Green, Robert, 1969–
  Skateboards / by Robert Green.
    p. cm. — (Global products)
  ISBN-13: 978-1-60279-023-0 (hardcover)
  ISBN-10: 1-60279-023-X (hardcover)
  1. Skateboard industry. 2. Skateboards. I. Title. II. Series.
  HD9993.S5182G74 2008
  338.4'7685362—dc22   2007003655

*Cherry Lake Publishing would like to acknowledge the work of
The Partnership for 21st Century Skills.
Please visit www.21stcenturyskills.org for more information.*

TABLE OF CONTENTS

CHAPTER ONE

SURFING ON LAND

Skateboarding is a great way to travel and get some exercise at the same time.

When bright-eyed Rosa Diaz flew into the kitchen on her new skateboard, she got the usual tongue-lashing from her mom. "How many times have I told you not to skate in the house, Rosa!"

Rosa had her headphones on, so she just watched her mom's lips move as she listened to her favorite music. But she had no doubt about the words being shouted. Her mom had a point. Grooves were starting to show in the wooden floor that her mother was so proud of. The wood was hard, but the skateboard was putting tiny nicks and dents into it.

As Rosa ate her pancake breakfast, she watched her mother making tortillas for dinner later that day. It was one of her favorite meals, and she started to feel bad about upsetting her mother. So, before she could cause any more headaches for her mom, she jumped up, flew out the door, and started cruising down the hill in front of her house toward school.

Southern California had a way of making days perfect for skate-boarders—warm and sunny, with gentle breezes. Besides, skateboarding was a good way to get to school, and it was Rosa's favorite hobby.

What Rosa didn't know was that much of her morning was centered on one particularly useful tree—the sugar maple. The tree was the source of the syrup that sweetened her pancakes. The hard wood, layered into **veneers**, was used for the floor her mother liked so much. And maple plywood, which is so good at holding its shape, is used to make most of the world's skateboards.

～

The skateboard traces its roots to Southern California. The earliest skateboards were made by attaching roller skate wheels to a narrow piece of wood. Surfers practiced balancing on these tricky boards on land, when

Trees give us one of our most useful of all building materials—wood.

Wood provides the frames for our houses and the boards for the floors we walk on. Much of our furniture is still made of wood and, of course, so too are most skateboards. Different types of wood come from different species of trees, and those species are located in forests all over the world.

What are some characteristics of wood that make is so useful?

the water was too calm to surf. Surfing is kind of like skateboarding on the sea, and skateboarding is a bit like surfing on land.

Skateboards are relatively simple objects. They are made of a deck, usually wood, on which the rider stands. The only other necessary parts are the **ball bearings**, the wheels, and the trucks, which are parts that hold the wheels to the deck.

Trucks attach the wheels to a skateboard's deck.

CHAPTER TWO

FROM THE MILL
TO THE FACTORY

Kids at an extreme sports camp in Pennsylvania
work on their skateboards.

As Rosa skateboarded past her local park on her way to school, she noticed construction workers unloading large pieces of wood. Rosa, with time to spare before getting to school, skated over to see what the workers were building.

"Hey, what's going on? Are you guys building something?" asked Rosa.

One of the construction workers looked down at her skateboard and smiled. "Yeah, we're constructing a new skateboard park."

Rosa screamed with excitement, drawing the attention of the other construction workers. She couldn't believe that a skate park was being built in her neighborhood.

Some communities have skateboard parks where skateboarders can gather to enjoy their sport.

"When will it be ready?" she asked.

The construction worker looked at the pieces of wood laying on the ground and answered, "I'm not sure. We have to wait for more wood to come in from the Northeast."

Rosa's face fell, but she was curious about the wood they needed. "Where does the wood come from? How do you get it here?"

The man began to explain the process of how wood is harvested from forests and turned into the material needed to create decks for skateboards and ramps for skateboarding parks.

❧

To make a skateboard deck that can take a beating and carry the weight of a person without warping, skateboard makers often turn to durable maple wood. Maple trees grow abundantly around the Great Lakes, and in the northeastern parts of Canada and the United States. The tree is so common in Canada that the maple leaf serves as a symbol of that country. The tree also grows in parts of Europe and Asia, but the variety with the hardest wood is most common in North America.

Maple trees are cut by loggers and shipped by truck to a mill. At the mill, plywood is **manufactured** in a process intended to make the tough maple into an even stronger piece of wood. Although the sugar maple is a hardwood tree, ideal for building, wood warps when pressure is placed on

A barker strips the bark from a log.

it or when it is exposed to moisture. Gluing thin sheets of wood together
into plywood makes the wood less likely to change shape or break.

To make plywood, a log is first stripped of its bark by a machine known
as a barker. The entire log is then conditioned by soaking it in hot water
or exposing it to steam. This makes it easier to peel off thin sheets of wood
with a machine known as a lathe. Each sheet is called a veneer or ply. The

sheets of veneer are then coated with glue and sandwiched together. The final step is to place the wood into a press that squeezes the layers of ply together and allows the glue to thoroughly soak into the wood.

The result is a very hard piece of wood, known as plywood. The key to its strength is that the **grain**—the natural lines in the wood—of each layer runs at right angles to the one above and below it. The grain runs lengthwise on the first sheet, side to side on the second, lengthwise on the third, and so on. This allows for each layer to increase the strength of the next in a crisscross fashion.

The number of layers of wood determines the thickness and toughness of the final product. Skateboards are usually made with seven-ply maple plywood—in other words, seven thick layers of wood are glued together to make the springy, hard board that can hold its shape and take a beating.

21st Century Content

Many people today are concerned about the environment. They try to buy products from companies that manufacture goods in ways that won't harm the environment. Smart business leaders respond to this by looking at their manufacturing processes and altering them to make consumers happy.

For example, many skateboard companies now use a water-based glue to make plywood for their decks. This type of glue sets without heat, so the plywood sets in a press that relies only on pressure. This type of glue is considered less harmful to the natural world around us and is therefore preferred as a "green" product—one that is more **environmentally friendly**.

CHAPTER THREE

ADDING MOTION

*It is important to wear a helmet and other
protective gear whenever you skateboard.*

"I get it. Plywood is the best kind of wood for skateboards and vert ramps in skate parks because it can hold its shape better," said Rosa.

"That's right!" the construction worker explained. "That's why we have to wait for the next shipment of plywood to come in before we can continue building. Hey kid, shouldn't you be in school?" Rosa looked down at her watch. She was five minutes late!

"Oh no, I have to get going! Thanks, see you later!" Rosa yelled, as she skated away toward school.

"Ah, Ms. Diaz, so nice of you to join us!" exclaimed Mrs. Woods as Rosa entered the classroom and tried to slip into her seat without being noticed.

Mrs. Woods continued her lesson. "Today, we are going to talk about the environment and ways in which companies are manufacturing goods with the environment in mind. Now I know that a lot of you skateboard to school, and today we are going to talk about how one skateboard manufacturer uses environmentally friendly methods to produce its skateboards."

"Mrs. Woods, which company is that?" asked Rosa.

"It is the Comet Skateboard Company. Does anyone in here own a Comet skateboard?" asked Mrs. Woods.

Five students raised their hands proudly, including Rosa. Mrs. Woods, amazed by the number of hands that shot up, continued. "Well then, you should all be happy to know that you are skateboarding on environmentally sound skateboards."

One of the students asked, "Mrs. Woods, how are these 'environmentally sound' skateboards made?"

Stacks of logs are ready for processing at a timber mill.

Mrs. Woods began to explain the process of skateboard manufacturing and how Comet Skateboard and other manufacturers keep the environment in mind.

◞

Skateboard manufacturers often make their own plywood with sheets of wood bought from timber mills. Comet Skateboard is a company that reflects the independent spirit of many small skateboard makers. Comet buys maple veneer from North American companies that practice sustainable harvesting. This means that the trees cut down for wood products are replaced through replanting. This is an environmentally friendly way of harvesting trees. Environmentally friendly manufacturers try to reduce the harm caused to the environment by manufacturing.

Comet, located in San Francisco, California, presses the maple veneer in its own high-pressure presses to make decks. Comet also uses other types of wood in its skateboards, such as bamboo, poplar, and hickory.

Once the veneer layers are pressed into a piece of plywood, a worker shapes the board by rounding the edges. At the Comet factory, this is done by a computer-controlled machine that ensures the boards are the same shape each time. Because Comet is concerned about the environment, the company now runs this machine on solar power. The sun's energy is converted into electricity, which then powers the machine that cuts and shapes the skateboards.

The final step in the creation of the deck is the finish—the paint and lacquer coating on the outside of the board. Skateboards are decorated with many different colors, patterns, and pictures. All of these must be applied in a way that ensures they won't chip, fade, or peel away when the skateboard is ridden.

Comet, like many other small skateboard makers around the world, designs and sells its own decks and wheels. Trucks, the metal parts that attach the wheels to the deck, are often made by different companies and sold separately.

The popular Girl Skateboard Company sells complete skateboards, with decks, wheels, trucks, and bearings. The company makes all the parts except for the trucks. Girl buys trucks from Royal, a company that specializes in making trucks and selling them to skateboard companies. This is known as **specialization**, a process that allows a manufacturer to become especially good at making just one part of a product.

Specialization is just one of the interesting aspects of the manufacturing process. In recent years, manufacturing has become truly global, with skateboard makers growing in size and spreading their factories around the world.

CHAPTER FOUR

A WIDENING PICTURE

*Shops that sell skateboard decks and wheels
often also sell parts for in-line skates.*

After school, Rosa headed to her favorite skateboarding shop. She loved stopping by the store and seeing all the new styles of boards, flashy new wheels, and stronger trucks.

"Hey, Rosa!" said Tommy, the man behind the counter. He had owned the skateboarding shop for 15 years and knew Rosa well.

"Hey, Tommy!" replied Rosa. "Did you get anything new in the store today?"

Tommy smiled as he reached under the counter. "Well, Rosa, it just so happens that we got in a whole new shipment of those Comet skateboards you like." He pulled out a brand-new, shiny Comet skateboard. "All-new design, glossing, and stronger plywood composite—a real beauty!"

Rosa's eyes opened wide as she stared at the skateboard. "Wow, Tommy! It looks amazing. Where did you get them from?" asked Rosa.

"We just got them in a shipment from China," he said.

"They can make Comet skateboards in China?!"

Tommy laughed. "Of course they can. Skateboarding may have its roots in Southern California, but skateboards can be made by people all over the world."

Another interesting feature of global manufacturing today is **outsourcing**. This refers to the use of workers in other countries to make products in factories. Foreign workers who earn lower **wages** are less expensive to employ than workers who demand higher wages.

The cost of **labor** is determined by various factors, such as the number of available workers. In China, the world's most populous country, workers are plentiful and labor is inexpensive. Like many other manufacturers, some skateboard makers have begun outsourcing labor to Chinese factories to keep prices low and maintain or increase **profits**.

One leading skateboard company that uses this business model is Dwindle Distribution. The company is one of the largest skateboard manufacturers in the world. They sell their products under seven brand names, which would be more familiar to the customer than the name of the parent company. Dwindle decided to move its factories to China to keep costs down and remain competitive.

The Pudong district in Shanghai, China, is a center of business activity.

Outsourcing is such a large part of global manufacturing that it is important to look at some of the reasons a company like Dwindle would turn to this model. Any company will weigh a number of factors before making a major change in its manufacturing process. One contributing factor is the cost of liability. Liability insurance covers those at risk of being sued for negligence. Skateboard manufacturers are sometimes sued when skateboard riders get hurt. The riders can hold the maker of the product that they were using when they were injured liable—in other words, legally responsible—and sue for damages in court. As a result, manufacturers of all sorts need to figure in the costs of legal fees for lawyers and lawsuits into their budgets.

This is just one contributing factor to the costs of doing business. Another major reason for moving factories abroad to lower costs is the increasing pressure placed on U.S. companies by manufacturers in Asia, who make products at a much lower cost. So far, there are still skateboard makers, such as

Dwindle, that are still making high-end skateboards, while the newer companies in Asia are producing lower-end skateboards. Yet, this competition still puts pressure on companies to cut costs, and one option is to use less-expensive workers in factories overseas.

Outsourcing of this type is controversial. On the one hand, jobs move to other countries, leaving unemployed workers behind. On the other hand, prices of the products made abroad are usually cheaper. This means that **consumers** pay less for these products in their local stores. From a global perspective, outsourcing also provides jobs for workers in other countries.

No matter how one feels about outsourcing, it is a very large part of the story of global manufacturing today. Dwindle is able to make more skateboards at a lower cost because of outsourcing. This allows the company to be more competitive, and competition lies at the heart of our **capitalist system.**

21st Century Content

China has attracted outsourcing jobs because of its large workforce and the low wages paid to factory workers there. But the Chinese government is also a part of the story. The government sometimes supports new businesses by giving them land and building roads and transportation facilities to and from their factories. Chinese government leaders believe that the increase of business in China will raise the level of prosperity for everyone.

CHAPTER FIVE

A GLOBAL FACTORY

Skateboard companies sell skateboard decks with many different designs.

Rosa was finally putting it all together. "I get it! So skateboards are really a global product, right?"

"Exactly right!" said Tommy.

Rosa, still eyeing that new skateboard, asked, "So how much does this one cost?"

"Fifty-five dollars," Tommy answered.

Rosa frowned. "I don't have that much money right now, but I sure would like to have that skateboard."

"You're one of my best customers, Rosa. Start saving your money, and maybe you'll have one of these skateboards sooner than you think!"

"Okay, Tommy. Now I have to head home. I'll see you soon," said Rosa as she skated out the door to head home to Mom, dinner, and homework.

When Rosa got home, she realized what she had to do. She stopped skating at the door, picked up her board, and walked into the house. Her mom was inside cooking dinner, but before she could say a word, Rosa started to apologize. "Mom, I'm sorry about skating in the house. I know now why you don't want me to, and I understand the importance of the wood we get for the floors and my skateboard."

Rosa's mom accepted the apology and then asked with a curious smile, "What exactly happened at school today?"

∾

Dwindle Distribution's outsourcing benefits consumers of skateboards and the workers in Chinese factories. But it would be a mistake to think that only Chinese laborers are making the skateboards.

The maple wood for Dwindle's Chinese factories still comes from North America. How is it that the company can have this wood shipped to a factory halfway around the world and still save money? The answer lies in an interesting economic phenomenon known as the economy of scale. As a company makes more of a product, the individual price of a

Containerships carry skateboards and other cargo across oceans.

unit drops. In other words, the more one makes of something, the less expensive it is to make.

This means Dwindle can afford the cost of sending maple from North America to China and still keep prices low, because they are making more and more skateboards. Because of the economy of scale, large companies tend to grow even larger.

So if a company outsources the production of its decks, just what does the company actually do? It designs skateboards, improving the technology and the look of the boards. It also distributes them, which means that the company arranges for the shipping of the skateboards from their factories in China to stores all over the world.

Although the factory workers are Chinese, the company employs many other people to handle distribution, design, marketing, and advertising. All of these are highly skilled jobs, requiring a good education and the ability to think through complicated problems. Distribution itself is a global enterprise that involves coordinating orders from customers and supplies from the factories. The Internet has made this process easier and faster than ever before.

It is also important to realize that not all of a company's jobs are going overseas. Dwindle,

If so many skateboards are made of maple plywood, what makes them unique? One answer is the design. People buy skateboards based partly on the way they look. Decorating skateboards has always been a big part of skateboard culture. Sometimes kids just cover them with stickers. Sometimes a company produces such interesting designs that people buy its skateboards just for their style. Can you think of some other ways that a company could make its skateboards different from other companies' skateboards?

for example, still employs many people at its **headquarters** in El Segundo, California, and through a global network of distributors.

Even Chinese factory workers making skateboards use machines that were made in advanced industrial countries, such as European nations, the United States, and Japan. The United States, in fact, is still a leading manufacturing center for machines that are used to make other products. So the Chinese factory itself is a consumer of American manufactured products. The making of machines is also a highly specialized form of manufacturing, and the workers who make them often earn very good salaries.

The picture of modern manufacturing stretches around the globe. Wood sails on ships from North America to China. In Chinese factories, Western machines are used to make skateboards. A worldwide network of distributors ships them to **markets** all around the globe. This is known as a division of labor—the use of different groups to perform different steps in the manufacturing process. At the end of this long voyage around the world is a consumer like Rosa Diaz, who just can't stay off her skateboard, whether she is in the house or out on the street.

～

"Sounds like you had a very educational day!" Rosa's mom exclaimed.

"You bet!" Rosa replied.

Her mom pulled out an opened envelope and said, "Rosa, before you go upstairs, we need to talk. I received your report card in the mail today. Is there anything you want to say?"

Rosa shook her head, scared of what was in that envelope.

Rosa's mom pulled out the slip in the envelope and smiled. "Straight A's! I am so proud of you." She gave Rosa a big hug and continued, "And because you did so well, I got you a little something this afternoon."

She reached behind the kitchen counter to reveal a shiny new Comet skateboard, just like the one Rosa had seen at the store.

"Wow, Mom! I don't know what to say. Thank you so much!" Rosa hugged her mom as hard as she could.

Rosa's mom said, "Your friend Tommy said that this skateboard was made in China. Did you know that?"

Rosa grinned and said, "Yes, Mom, I know!"

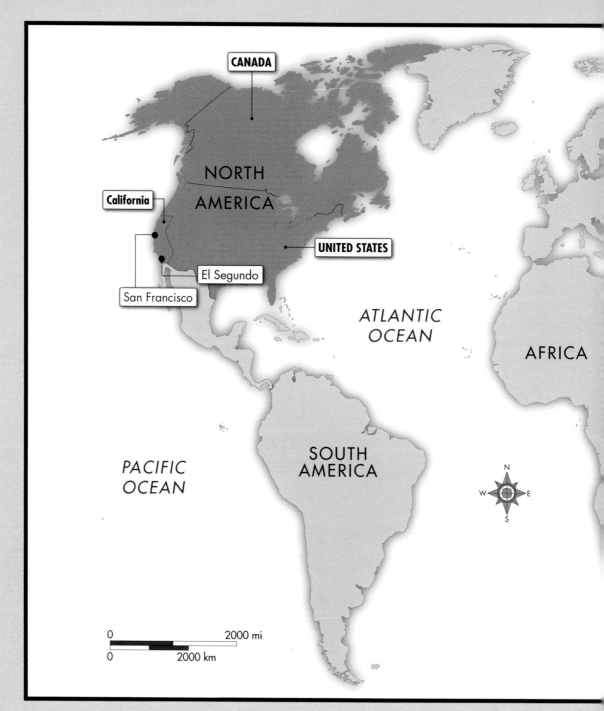

This map shows the countries and cities mentioned in the text.

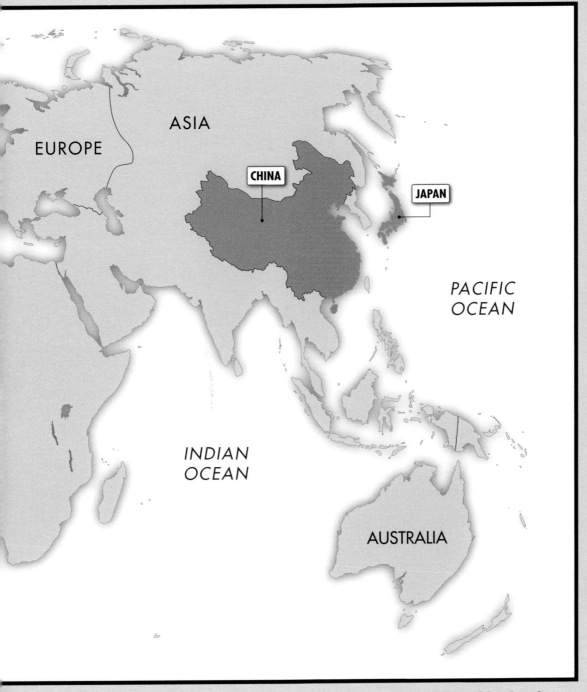

They are the locations of some of the companies involved in the making and selling of skateboards.

Glossary

ball bearings (BAWL BAIR-ingz) a machine part in which one part rolls upon loose steel balls to minimize the effects of friction

capitalist system (KAP-uh-tuh-list SISS-tuhm) an economy in which production and distribution are controlled by private companies that compete for consumers and sell their good(s) in a competitive market

consumers (kuhn-SOO-murz) people who buy and use products and services

environmentally friendly (en-VYE-ruhn-MENT-uhl-lee FREND-lee) adopting practices that intend to limit damage caused to the environment by human activity

grain (GRAYN) the texture or pattern produced by the fibers in a piece of wood

labor (LAY-bur) a group of workers who work for wages

manufactured (man-yuh-FAK-churd) to make something, usually on a large scale

markets (MAR-kits) places where goods are sold

outsourcing (OUT-sorss-ing) the use of foreign labor to make products for a domestic company

profits (PROF-its) the amount of money left after all the costs of running a business have been subtracted from the money made from selling goods or services

specialization (SPESH-uh-li-ZA-shun) the act of focusing on a particular part of a process

veneers (vuh-NEARZ) thin sheets of wood

wages (WAY-jez) the money paid to a worker by an employer

For More Information

Books

Davis, James. *Skateboarding Is Not a Crime: 50 Years of Street Culture*. Buffalo, NY: Firefly Books, 2004.

Hoye, Jacob, (editor). *Boards: The Art and Design of the Skateboard*. New York: Universe, 2003.

Segovia, Patty, and Rebecca Heller. *Skater Girl: A Girl's Guide to Skateboarding*. Berkeley, CA: Ulysses Press, 2006.

Web Sites

Exploratorium.edu—Skateboard Science
www.exploratorium.edu/skateboarding/index.html
For a look at the science behind skateboarding

Kidzworld.com—How to Build a Quarter Pipe
www.kidzworld.com/article/4724-how-to-build-a-quarter-pipe
Instructions for building your own backyard quarter pipe

INDEX

ABOUT THE AUTHOR

Robert Green is the author of three other books in this series—*MP3 Players, Cars,* and *Bicycles*—and many other books for young adults. He holds graduate degrees from New York University and Harvard. He learned a great deal about globalization while living in Taiwan, where he studied Chinese and worked for the Taiwanese government.